SPORTS GOATs:
THE GREATEST OF ALL TIME

GOATs OF
TENNIS

BY KAREN PRICE

SportsZone

An Imprint of Abdo Publishing
abdobooks.com

T0019746

abdobooks.com

Published by Abdo Publishing, a division of ABDO, PO Box 398166, Minneapolis, Minnesota 55439. Copyright © 2022 by Abdo Consulting Group, Inc. International copyrights reserved in all countries. No part of this book may be reproduced in any form without written permission from the publisher. SportsZone™ is a trademark and logo of Abdo Publishing.

Printed in the United States of America, North Mankato, Minnesota.
102021
012022

Cover Photo: Anja Niedringhaus/AP Images
Interior Photos: AP Images, 4, 5, 8–9, 9; Bob Martin/Allsport/Getty Images Sport/Getty Images, 6–7, 7; Mark Lennihan/AP Images, 10, 11; Daily Express/Hulton Archive/Getty Images, 12, 12–13; Al Messerschmidt/AP Images, 14, 14–15; Adam Stoltman/AP Images, 16, 16–17, 20–21, 21, 22–23, 23; Malcolm Clarke/AP Images, 18–19, 19; Elise Amendola/AP Images, 24–25, 25, 30–31, 31; Jon Simon/Bettmann/Getty Images, 26, 27; Stuart Robinson/Express Newspapers/AP Images, 28–29, 29; Hans Deryk/AP Images, 32, 32–33; Fabian Bimmer/AP Images, 34, 35; Vincent Thian/AP Images, 36, 36–37; Clive Mason/Getty Images Sport/Getty Images, 38–39, 39; Darko Vojinovic/AP Images, 40–41; Mike Egerton/AP Images, 42, 42–43

Editor: Charlie Beattie
Series Designer: Jake Nordby

Library of Congress Control Number: 2021941704

Publisher's Cataloging-in-Publication Data

Names: Price, Karen, author.
Title: GOATs of tennis / by Karen Price
Description: Minneapolis, Minnesota : Abdo Publishing, 2022 | Series: Sports GOATs: The greatest of all time | Includes online resources and index.
Identifiers: ISBN 9781532196546 (lib. bdg.) | ISBN 9781644947142 (pbk.) | ISBN 9781098218355 (ebook)
Subjects: LCSH: Tennis--Juvenile literature. | Tennis players--Juvenile literature. | Tennis--Records--Juvenile literature. | Professional athletes--Juvenile literature.
Classification: DDC 796.342--dc23

TABLE OF CONTENTS

ROD LAVER

In 1960 and 1961, Rod Laver reached the finals in six of the eight major tennis tournaments. He won only two of them. But 1962 was his year. Laver won all four major tournaments, known as Grand Slams, becoming just the second men's player to accomplish a feat known as the calendar Grand Slam. His opponents were unable to compete with Laver's serve-and-volley skill. They took only four sets across the four final matches.

Born in Australia, the man they called the Rocket was only 24 in 1962. He had many good years of tennis left in him. But in the early 1960s, only amateur players were allowed to compete in the Grand Slam tournaments. Laver became ineligible the moment he turned professional in 1963.

Tennis began what is called the Open Era in 1968. This allowed professionals back into the Grand Slam events. The next year Laver cruised through the first three majors, leaving only the US Open. In those days, the tournament was played on grass, and rain made the surface slippery. Fellow Australian Tony Roche beat Laver 7–9 in the first set. Laver then changed his shoes from sneakers to spikes and lost only five more games on his way to victory.

FAST FACT

The first person to win all four Grand Slam championships in one year was American Don Budge in 1938. The second to achieve the calendar Grand Slam, and the first woman, was US player Maureen Connolly in 1953.

Since that year, no male player has accomplished the Grand Slam. And Laver remains the only player, male or female, to do it twice. The stadium in Melbourne, where the Australian Open final is played, was renamed Rod Laver Arena in 2000.

Rod Laver poses with the championship trophy after defeating American Chuck McKinley in straight sets at the 1961 Wimbledon final.

Billie Jean King stretches for a backhand at Wimbledon in 1982. King played singles in the prestigious tournament 21 times and won six titles.

BILLIE JEAN KING

Billie Jean King started playing tennis in Long Beach, California, at the age of 11 in 1954. Soon after, she told her mother she would be the No. 1 player in the world someday. After a slow start to a career that began in 1959, King eventually reached the top spot in 1966. She would spend most of the next six years ranked No. 1.

A player who thrived in singles, doubles, and mixed doubles, King won 39 Grand Slam tournament titles in all. She had the most success at Wimbledon, where she racked up six singles and 14 doubles wins. In 1967 she won the singles, doubles, and mixed doubles at the London, England-based tournament. She then matched the feat two months later at the US Championships, the tournament that in 1968 became the US Open.

One of King's most notable moments happened outside of tournament tennis. In 1973 she beat men's player Bobby Riggs in an exhibition match. The event was watched by 90 million fans on TV as well as a sellout crowd in the Astrodome, where Houston's baseball and football teams played. It was seen as a major milestone for women's sports.

King's activism for women in sports went far beyond beating Riggs. She was one of the first to champion equal pay for female athletes. She also became an icon for the LGBTQ community when she came out as gay in 1981. Nearly three decades later, in 2009, she was awarded the Presidential Medal of Freedom by President Barack Obama.

Margaret Court holds up the Venus Rosewater Dish after defeating Billie Jean King in the 1970 Wimbledon Final.

MARGARET COURT

Some players excel as singles players. Some are better at doubles. Margaret Court was good at both. The only player who could stop Margaret Court from 1960 to 1975 seemed to be Court herself.

Born Margaret Smith, she dominated the amateur circuit from 1960 to 1966. Using her 5-foot-9-inch height and exceptional reach, she won the Australian Championships, later known as the Australian Open, each of those seven years as well as six other major titles.

She didn't win any of the four majors in 1968. But she would headline women's tennis for the next two years. Starting with the 1969 Australian Open, Court won eight of the next nine major tournaments. Rivals rarely challenged her during the run. Court lost only three sets total. After outlasting Billie Jean King 14–12, 11–9 at the 1970 Wimbledon final, she completed the Grand Slam by winning the US Open in three sets over Rosemary Casals. No woman would match that feat for another 18 years. Court came closer than anyone in 1973. She won three of the four, losing only in the semifinals at Wimbledon.

Court's career slowed down as she gave birth to four children in the 1970s. But when she finally retired in 1977, she had racked up 64 Grand Slam championships between singles, doubles, and mixed doubles. Like her fellow Australian Laver, she was honored when Show Court One at the Australian Open was renamed Margaret Court Arena in 2003.

JIMMY CONNORS

Jimmy Connors liked being an outsider. He once said he wasn't playing to make friends; he was playing to win. That showed in his frequent arguments with umpires, other players, and even crowds. Tennis fans of the 1970s and 1980s either loved or hated him. But whether he was playing the hero or villain, Connors won an awful lot.

A native of southern Illinois, Connors turned professional in 1972. Two years later he showed his supreme skill by posting a record of 99–4 for the year. He also won three of the four majors. Any chance to win a Grand Slam was lost when the French Open banned him for his involvement in an unrecognized professional league called World Team Tennis. The ban lasted only one year, but Connors chose not to return to Paris until 1979.

The 1970s were filled with great players, but few could top Connors from 1974 to 1978. He held the No. 1 ranking for 160 straight weeks, the longest of any player up to that point. The record stood for more than 30 years.

In 1991 Connors had not won a major in eight years and was ranked 174th in the world. He turned 39 during the US Open. Nonetheless he put on one last magical run to the semifinals. After often jeering Connors

FAST FACT

The US Open has been played on grass, clay, and hard courts over the years. Jimmy Connors is the only person to win on all three.

in the past, this time the New York crowd cheered him enthusiastically as he took down several younger opponents.

In addition to his success, Connors also innovated how the game was played. He was one of the first to use a metal racket over wood. And his ferocious two-handed backhand was a direct influence on the powerful tennis played by men's players today.

Jimmy Connors celebrates his quarterfinal victory during his improbable run at the 1991 US Open.

EVONNE GOOLAGONG CAWLEY

Several Australians, including Rod Laver and Margaret Court, dominated tennis in the 1960s. Evonne Goolagong Cawley came along in the early 1970s and added a unique twist to that heritage. She was born Evonne Goolagong as one of eight children in a Wiradjuri Aboriginal family. As Evonne grew up, the Goolagong family experienced poverty. Their home had dirt floors and no electricity. Evonne's first tennis racket was made from a wooden fruit box.

By 1971, at age 19, she was challenging Court in the Australian Open final. Court won, but Goolagong would take the next two majors that year. She won the French Open over fellow Australian Helen Gourlay then beat Court at Wimbledon.

The woman nicknamed Sunshine Supergirl for her graceful style and carefree nature reached six consecutive Australian Open finals starting in 1971. She won the tournament every year from 1974 to 1976. She missed the tournament in January of 1977 but won it when it was held again that December.

Goolagong Cawley's career was interrupted when she and her husband started a family. She played in only four tournaments from 1977 to 1979. But she made a triumphant return at Wimbledon in 1980. Goolagong Cawley beat American Chris Evert in the final. That made her the first mother to win the tournament in 66 years. The nine-year gap between Wimbledon titles was also the longest in tournament history.

Goolagong Cawley won seven Grand Slam singles titles in her career. She added seven more in doubles before retiring for good in 1983.

Evonne Goolagong Cawley stretches for a backhand during her 6–4, 6–1 victory over fellow Australian Margaret Court at the 1971 Wimbledon final.

CHRIS EVERT

Chris Evert was always cool and calm under pressure. That's why they called her the Ice Maiden. She rarely made mistakes and never seemed to get rattled. Even when she was down in a match, she was never out. And she never seemed to lose.

The Florida-born Evert was only 16 and still an amateur when she made her major debut at the US Open in 1971. No one expected her to do much damage. But Evert came from behind in three matches to reach the semifinals. She showed fans what was to come. Evert lasting deep into tournaments became the standard. In 49 majors entered between 1971 and 1987, Evert failed to reach the semis only once.

Before Evert most players tried to get to the net and play volleys as often as possible. Evert stayed back and placed accurate shots all over the court. Her two-handed backhand was especially tough. Opponents also struggled to get shots past her. She became known as the human backboard.

After capturing her first Grand Slam tournament title at the 1974 French Open, Evert won at least one of the Grand Slam events every year until 1987. That 13-year streak set an Open Era record.

Evert was at her best on clay courts and won a record seven French Open titles. At one point in her career, Evert won 125 straight matches on clay.

When she finally retired, Evert had won 18 major singles titles. Even more impressive was her record of 1,309–146. That .900 winning percentage is the best by any man or woman ever to step on a professional court.

Chris Evert played her first senior tournament at age 14 in 1969. She played her last in 1989.

BJORN BORG

Swede Bjorn Borg was such a star in the 1970s that his popularity even had its own name. They called it "Borgmania." He was known for his good looks. Borg had long, blond hair and kept it down with stylish striped headbands. But he wasn't just flash. Borg was a fierce opponent on the court.

He won his first major in 1974, taking the French Open when he was just 18. He won it again in 1975. Later he would add four more wins in Paris from 1978 to 1981. That streak was the longest in tournament history until Rafael Nadal won his fifth straight in 2014.

But it was at Wimbledon where Borg was at his best. For 41 matches between 1976 and the 1981 final, he was unbeatable on the grass surface. His string of five titles from 1976 to 1980 is tied for the longest win streak at Wimbledon. His five-set win over American John McEnroe in the 1980 Wimbledon final is considered by many to be the best men's match of all time.

Borg rarely showed his emotions on the court. But he was a fiery competitor who hated losing. He would often be silent for days after a defeat. He also grew tired of the constant attention from fans. It eventually led him to retire in 1983, when he was only 26. At the time of his retirement, his 11 major titles were an Open Era record.

FAST FACT

In 1979 Bjorn Borg became the first player to earn $1 million in prize money in one season. By comparison, Novak Djokovic won an all-time record $21,646,145 in 2015.

Bjorn Borg drops to his knees to celebrate his victory over John McEnroe in the 1980 Wimbledon final.

Martina Navratilova played in 32 Grand Slam singles finals over the course of her career.

MARTINA NAVRATILOVA

In 1983 Martina Navratilova was dominating the women's tour. Her record that year was 86–1. At one point, she won a record 74 matches in a row. Legendary tennis commentator Bud Collins suggested the sport create a "higher league" for Navratilova.

Using an aggressive serve-and-volley strategy, Navratilova won more major titles than any other player. In addition to her 18 singles titles, Navratilova was also an unmatched doubles player. She won 31 women's doubles major titles and 10 more in mixed doubles.

Navratilova started playing in Grand Slam tournaments in 1973, at age 16, representing her native Czechoslovakia. But she fled the country's communist government in 1975 and settled in the United States. She was eventually granted US citizenship in 1981.

That was also the same year she began taking over the tennis circuit. A late bloomer, Navratilova had only two major singles titles by age 25. Between 1981 and 1987, she won 15 more, including six consecutive titles at Wimbledon. Though she did not win all four major tournaments in the same year, Navratilova once held all four at the same time. She won Wimbledon and the US Open in 1983 then opened 1984 with wins at the Australian and French Opens.

Navratilova's rivalry with Evert is considered one of the best in tennis history. The two met in 14 major finals, with Navratilova winning 10. Despite their heated competition on the court, Navratilova and Evert were very close friends off it. They frequently practiced together and even won doubles titles together at the French Open and Wimbledon early in their careers.

Ivan Lendl sets up for a backhand during his championship run at the 1986 US Open.

IVAN LENDL

In the late 1970s and early 1980s, players with big personalities like Jimmy Connors and John McEnroe made most of the headlines in men's tennis. Czechoslovakia-born Ivan Lendl was quieter, but he was just as intimidating. His lethal forehand and icy demeanor earned him the nicknames the Terminator and Ivan the Terrible.

While other players attacked the net, Lendl stayed on the baseline and crushed the ball. He was known for his use of topspin, which kept his shots low and also made them incredibly fast. After winning his first major title at the French Open in 1984, he went on to win seven more by 1990.

Perhaps Lendl could have won even more tournaments had his career not overlapped with several other great players. He lost 11 major finals. Seven of those losses came to fellow greats Bjorn Borg, Connors, McEnroe, and Boris Becker. Nonetheless he was still ranked No. 1 for 270 weeks in his career, including 157 straight at one point.

Lendl was a pioneer in training, nutrition, and fitness for players. Few players in Lendl's era made adjustments to their equipment. But he constantly tinkered with his racket to make it more effective. Modern players have continued this trend.

A bad back forced Lendl to retire in 1994. But his impact is still felt by those who play the game today. Many of them play at the baseline like he did. Lendl also became a successful coach. He famously guided Scottish star Andy Murray to the No. 1 world ranking and two major titles in 2012 and 2013.

John McEnroe returns a shot during the US Open in 1980. McEnroe went on to win the tournament, beating Bjorn Borg in a five-set final.

JOHN MCENROE

John McEnroe has always been a talker. Today he is a respected tennis commentator on television. But during his playing career, his mouth often got him into trouble. The New Yorker's play usually got him out of it.

McEnroe was famous for his on-court tantrums. He earned the nickname Super Brat by frequently yelling at umpires. One of his go-to lines was to yell, "You cannot be serious!" if he disagreed with a call. It would later become the title of his autobiography.

Through all the yelling, McEnroe was winning. On the court, he was considered an artist with great talent and skill. McEnroe became the youngest US Open champion in 31 years in 1979, when he was only 20. That was his first major win. He would go on to add six more. He was ranked No. 1 in the world at the end of each year from 1981 to 1984.

McEnroe's best year came in 1984. He won 62 of 69 sets in major tournaments. At Wimbledon he won the entire tournament while only losing one set. He finished the tournament by whipping rival Jimmy Connors 6–1, 6–1, 6–2 in the final. McEnroe capped off the year by beating Ivan Lendl in straight sets at the US Open.

After struggling in 1985, McEnroe took time away from tennis. He returned in late 1986 but was never able to regain his championship form. But for six years from 1979 to 1984, he was the most feared man on the court by fellow players and umpires alike.

Steffi Graf's 377 weeks at No. 1 in the world rankings is an Open-Era record.

STEFFI GRAF

The dominant careers of Chris Evert and Martina Navratilova were winding down in the late 1980s. Steffi Graf was a big reason why. The young West German's career was taking off. She would go on to rule women's tennis for a decade.

Graf burst onto the scene in 1987 when she beat Navratilova to win the French Open. She was just 17 at the time. But it was in 1988 that Graf truly took over. And she did it in historic fashion.

At the Australian Open that year, Graf knocked off Evert in the final. She then won the French Open final without dropping a single game. Wimbledon was a tougher test. Graf dropped the first set to Navratilova but came back to win. She then took the US Open in three sets over Gabriela Sabatini. With that, Graf became the first calendar Grand Slam singles winner since Margaret Court in 1970. No player, female or male, has done it since.

But Graf's historic year was not over. Graf headed to Seoul, South Korea, to compete in the 1988 Summer Olympics. She came home with the gold medal, again beating Sabatini. Graf's five titles in one year coined a new term: the Golden Slam.

Graf would capture at least one major every year until 1997. In 1999 she won the French Open in three sets over Switzerland's Martina Hingis. It was Graf's twenty-second and final Grand Slam tournament title. After an injury ended her season in August of that year, she decided to retire from tennis. She left the game as perhaps the greatest women's player ever.

ANDRE AGASSI

Loud, bold, and confident were just some of the words used to describe Andre Agassi in the late 1980s and early '90s. Superstar was another. His rock-star looks and big personality led to fame and many endorsement deals.

His early results didn't always match his image. The Las Vegas–born Agassi made only three Grand Slam finals his first six years on tour and lost them all. But he broke through at Wimbledon in 1992 for his first major win. Two years later he won his first US Open. He then won the Australian Open for the first time in 1995, giving him victories in back-to-back majors.

At the 1996 Olympics in Atlanta, Agassi made history by becoming the first American man to win the singles gold medal since 1924. But his play suffered for the next two years due to injuries and personal problems. Many people thought Agassi was finished as a top player. At one point, he dropped to No. 141 in the world rankings.

In 1999 Agassi staged a comeback. Down two sets at the French Open final, he rallied to win. In doing so, he became the first men's player to win the career Grand Slam since Rod Laver. After a loss in the Wimbledon final to longtime rival Pete Sampras, Agassi won again at the

FAST FACT

Tennis power couple Andre Agassi and Steffi Graf married in 2001 and have two children, son Jaden Gil and daughter Jaz Elle. Jaden carried on his parents' athleticism by playing baseball at the University of Southern California.

US Open. This time he rallied from behind to defeat another American, Todd Martin.

Back injuries finally forced his retirement in 2006. He gave the announcement on the court after losing in the third round of the US Open. The New York crowd responded with a four-minute ovation for one of tennis' most colorful players.

Andre Agassi shows off his powerful forehand, and his unique fashion sense, at the US Open early in his career.

Pete Sampras once held the men's singles record for most Grand Slam wins with 14. The previous record of 12 had been held by Roy Emerson for 33 years.

Pete Sampras returns a shot during the Wimbledon final in 2000. The tournament victory was Sampras's seventh in eight years at the All England Club.

PETE SAMPRAS

Men's tennis in the 1990s was Pete Sampras on one level and everyone else a cut below. Pistol Pete burst onto the scene as a 19-year-old in 1990, beating Ivan Lendl and Andre Agassi at the US Open and becoming the tournament's youngest winner. He remained at the top of the sport for the next 12 years.

Sampras attacked his opponents right away. The Californian was one of the most effective servers of all time. Though his serve was not the hardest, he made up for it with incredible accuracy. Most players slow down their second serves. Sampras rarely did. As a result, he was extremely tough to beat on his service games.

That strategy helped him dominate from 1993 to 2000. He won at least one major every year during that stretch. He was ranked No. 1 in the world at the end of the year every year from 1993 to 1998.

Despite facing many top opponents at Grand Slam tournaments over the years, Sampras rarely lost a major final. He finished his career with a 14–4 record in major championship matches. He even won eight in a row at one point. Sampras was at his best at Wimbledon. He won on the grass surface seven times in eight years starting in 1993.

The 2002 US Open was Sampras's last tournament. He came in seeded 17th. But Sampras battled his way to the final against Agassi. He knocked off his longtime rival in four sets to go out on top.

Monica Seles powers a forehand on her way to winning the US Open in 1991.

MONICA SELES

For three years in the early 1990s, Monica Seles was the center of the tennis world. And she was still just a teenager. The young Yugoslavian looked set for a long career of dominance, but one of tennis' most frightening incidents took Seles off the court. It also may have robbed tennis of a great rivalry.

Steffi Graf had won eight of the previous nine Grand Slam tournaments heading into the 1990 French Open. Seles was just 16, but she shocked the tennis world in the final by beating Graf in straight sets for her first major title.

Seles won seemingly everything for the next two years. She captured the Australian, French, and US Opens in 1991. Only a shin injury kept her out of Wimbledon and denied her a chance at a Grand Slam. Seles won everything but Wimbledon again in 1992, losing to Graf in London.

When Seles beat Graf in the 1993 Australian Open final, the rivalry was on. But Seles was playing in Germany later that year when a violent fan jumped out of the crowd during a match and stabbed her in the back. He claimed to be a fan of Graf's, and he hoped that injuring Seles would put his favorite player back on top.

Seles did not play again for two years. Upon returning she never again found her top form. The 1995 US Open was her first major tournament since the attack. It ended with a loss to Graf in the final. Seles won only one more major, the 1996 Australian Open, before her career ended in 2003.

MARTINA HINGIS

Many of the game's greats found huge success as teenagers. Martina Hingis may have been the biggest prodigy the sport has ever seen.

Hingis was named after Martina Navratilova and played like her too. Both covered the court with great athleticism. But while Navratilova had to wait until her mid-20s to reach the top, Hingis did so at an age when most people are starting high school.

At 15 she won her first major title, taking home the Wimbledon doubles championship in 1996. That made her the youngest player to ever win a major.

The next year, she added her first singles title, becoming the youngest Australian Open winner ever. After a loss in the French Open final, Hingis captured both Wimbledon and the US Open. She made it four out of five majors by taking the 1998 Australian Open championship as well. By then she was the youngest player ever to be ranked No. 1.

Sadly, ankle injuries began to undermine her career. Hingis won the Australian Open again in 1999 and made the final of that tournament in each of the next three years. But she would never win another singles major. She retired in 2002 at the age of 22. Though she came back twice, she never reached another final in singles.

Hingis also had great doubles success. She even won a calendar Grand Slam in doubles in 1998, a year after she nearly did it in singles. Many still wonder how many tournaments she would have won if she had been fully healthy.

Martina Hingis won three of the four Grand Slam tournaments as a 16-year-old in 1997.

VENUS WILLIAMS

Tall and strong from a young age, Venus Williams became known early on for her blazing serve and forceful ground strokes. Anyone who played against her needed to be ready for her power. For many years, few were.

Though she was singled out for stardom from the age of 12, Williams was unseeded when she entered the US Open in 1997. She advanced to the final before losing to Martina Hingis. Nonetheless she became the first unseeded player to make it that far in the Open Era. It was also the beginning of a great rivalry with Hingis and a sign of Williams's emerging talent.

Williams broke through for good in 2000. She won Wimbledon and the US Open that year, both in straight sets. The next year, she won both again, defeating her younger sister Serena Williams in the US Open final.

Though Williams never returned to that level of dominance again, she claimed three more Wimbledon wins by 2008. If it were not for Serena, Venus may have had a few more championships. Through 2021 Venus had lost nine times in major finals. Seven of those losses came against her younger sister.

FAST FACT

Venus Williams is tied with Kathleen McKane of Great Britain for the most Olympic medals of any tennis athlete, with five (four gold, one silver). Her sister, Serena, is third with four, all gold. The Williams sisters won doubles gold together in 2000, 2008, and 2012.

Williams displayed resilience in her long career. She battled injuries and a condition called Sjogren's syndrome, which would leave her tired, short of breath, and aching. Still she reached the final of the Australian Open at age 36 and Wimbledon at age 37. And she continued to compete as she entered her 40s.

In addition to her seven singles victories, Venus Williams has 14 Grand Slam doubles titles.

SERENA WILLIAMS

Serena Williams joined the professional circuit in 1995, the year after her older sister Venus Williams debuted. By the mid-2000s, she had passed Venus as the world's most dominant player. She would go on to surpass just about everyone else in tennis history.

Most top tennis players hone their skills at private tennis academies as children. The Williams sisters instead grew up playing on public courts in Compton, California. They overcame many disadvantages on their paths to greatness. As Black women, they also battled racism in a mostly white sport. The sisters became icons for aspiring players of color in the United States.

Serena beat her older sister to a Grand Slam tournament title, winning the US Open in 1999. Before long a Williams sister would be appearing in nearly every major final. Often they would face each other. Between June 2002 and January 2003, the Williams sisters met in all four major finals. Serena won them all. As Serena held all four major titles at the same time, the media dubbed the feat the Serena Slam.

It took six more years for Serena to return to that level of dominance. From 2009 to 2017, she won 14 major tournaments. She again held all four titles at the same time from 2014 to 2015. A chance at a Grand Slam ended in a disappointing three-set loss at the 2015 US Open semifinals. Her final win of the decade, at the 2017 Australian Open, was historic. It was Serena's 23rd Open Era major championship, surpassing the record held by Steffi Graf. She also beat sister Venus in the final, their ninth championship meeting.

FAST FACT

Venus and Serena Williams are undefeated in Grand Slam doubles finals together. They won their first at the French Open in 1999 and their 14th at Wimbledon in 2016.

As of July 2021, Serena Williams's $94.5 million in career prize money was more than twice that of any other women's player.

Roger Federer was ranked No. 1 in the world from February 4, 2004, to August 17, 2008, a record 237 weeks in a row.

ROGER FEDERER

Men's tennis experienced a golden era in the 2000s. Three players led the way, including Spain's Rafael Nadal and Serbia's Novak Djokovic. But Switzerland's Roger Federer came first. For two decades, he set standards his rivals had to match.

Federer was a threat on all surfaces, but he was at his best at Wimbledon. His powerful serve, quick groundstrokes, and slicing backhand worked well on the speedy grass surface. Federer captured his first title there as a 21-year-old in 2003. It was the start of a run of six Wimbledon titles in seven years.

During that stretch, Federer played in 20 of 23 Grand Slam finals. Three times he reached all four in the same year. Rod Laver had been the last man to accomplish that. While Federer won multiple Australian and US Opens, the French Open remained out of his reach. Nadal ruled the tournament and beat Federer in three straight finals between 2006 and 2008.

In 2009 Nadal was upset in the fourth round by Robin Soderling. That opened the door for Federer. He beat Soderling in straight sets in the final. Federer had completed the Career Slam. He also had tied Pete Sampras's record of 14 men's Grand Slam titles. Federer broke the record a month later at Wimbledon and had 20 total titles entering 2022.

Men's players in previous eras rarely contended for titles after turning 30. Federer set a new standard for longevity. He reached eight major finals after his 30th birthday and won four. His 2017 Wimbledon title made him the tournament's oldest winner ever at 35 years, 11 months.

RAFAEL NADAL

Many statues are built after great players retire. The French Open built one of Rafael Nadal while he was still at the top of his game. It was installed on May 27, 2021. Five days later, the 35-year-old played his opening match. It was a fitting tribute to the dominance of the man nicknamed the King of Clay.

Surprisingly, Nadal did not win the 2021 French Open. The loss was just his fourth at the tournament since he first won it as a teenager in 2005. In one of those, he was forced out due to injury before the third round. Simply put, no player has ruled one event as completely as Nadal in Paris.

The Spanish lefthander's game was perfect for the clay surface. He used his powerful forehands to back opponents up. Then he would place soft drop shots just over the net or powerful winners out wide. Defensively he covered the entire court with blinding speed. Opponents found it tough to get shots past him.

Rivals Novak Djokovic and Roger Federer had to prove they could beat the king on clay. But Nadal had to prove to critics that he could win the other big tournaments. After six years of trying, he finally upset Federer at Wimbledon in 2008. All doubters were silenced after Nadal

FAST FACT

Tennis has been an Olympic medal sport since 1988. The only men to win all four Grand Slam tournaments plus an Olympic gold medal in their careers are Andre Agassi and Rafael Nadal.

took home the 2009 Australian Open. He completed the Career Slam by winning the US Open in 2010, one month after a second Wimbledon win.

Nadal's French Open win in 2020 matched Federer's record of 20 Grand Slam tournament wins. It was his 13th victory on Paris clay in 17 tries.

Rafael Nadal takes a bite out of La Coupe des Mousquetaires after winning the French Open in 2014, his ninth victory in ten years at the prestigious tournament.

NOVAK DJOKOVIC

Roger Federer and Rafael Nadal dominated men's tennis during the early 2000s. Novak Djokovic was one of the few who managed to win anything during that stretch. Over the next decade, however, the Serbian made sure tennis's dynamic duo became the Big Three.

One year younger than Nadal and six years younger than Federer, Djokovic took longer to break through at a major tournament. Nadal and Federer had combined to win 11 straight Grand Slams before Djokovic won his first at the 2008 Australian Open.

Using one of the game's best backhands and a powerful baseline stroke, Djokovic quickly climbed the victory leaderboard. In 2011 he won three of the four majors. He did it again in 2015, only missing out on the calendar Grand Slam through a loss to Nadal at the French Open. By the end of 2021, Djokovic had won 20 Grand Slam singles titles. That equaled Federer and Nadal for the men's record.

For as good as Djokovic was during the 2010s, he had one of his best seasons ever in 2021. He opened the season by winning his record ninth Australian Open, and fourth in a row. Then, after turning 34, he won the French Open and Wimbledon. That made him the first man since Rod Laver in 1969 to win the first three majors of the year. His quest to become the third man to win the calendar Grand Slam fell short when he lost in the US Open final. Once again, though, Djokovic had shown why he's not just part of the Big Three, but one of the sport's best ever.

Novak Djokovic is the only man in the Open Era to have won each Grand Slam tournament at least twice.

HONORABLE MENTIONS

HELEN WILLS

The Californian won 180 matches in a row from 1927 to 1933. She finished her career with 19 Grand Slam singles titles.

DON BUDGE

Budge became the first player ever to win a calendar Grand Slam in 1938. He is still the only American man to achieve that milestone.

MAUREEN CONNOLLY

The first woman ever to win a calendar Grand Slam in 1953, Connolly earned nine major singles titles before a horseback riding accident ended her career in 1954 at the age of 19.

ROY EMERSON

The Australian won 12 major championship singles titles between 1961 and 1971. He remains the only man to complete a career Grand Slam in both singles and doubles.

ARTHUR ASHE

During his 20-year career from 1959 to 1979, Ashe was the first Black man to win the US Open, Wimbledon, and Australian Open. He was also an activist for civil rights and equality in the United States and abroad.

ARANTXA SANCHEZ-VICARIO

Sanchez-Vicario was one of only 14 women ever to play in the singles finals of all four majors. The Spaniard won four major singles titles and was a five-time Olympian during the 1980s and 1990s.

LINDSAY DAVENPORT

A year-end No. 1 four times between 1998 and 2005, the hard-hitting American won three major singles titles and an Olympic gold medal.

ANDY MURRAY

Playing alongside fellow greats Federer, Nadal, and Djokovic, the Scotsman reached 11 major finals between 2008 and 2016, winning three.

GLOSSARY

aboriginal
Relating to the Indigenous peoples of Australia, who have lived there since before Europeans arrived.

amateur
A person who plays a sport without getting paid.

backhand
A shot in which the player swings from the opposite side of his or her body from the hand holding the racket.

baseline
The line at each end of a tennis court.

Grand Slam
The four most prestigious events in tennis; also refers to winning all four events in one year.

forehand
A swing at the ball on the same side of the body as the athlete's dominant hand.

Open Era
The current era of tennis that began in 1968 when both professionals and amateurs were allowed to compete in the four major championships. Prior to 1968, only amateurs could compete.

prodigy
A young player who has a great natural ability for a sport.

professional
A person who gets paid to perform.

serve
A shot that starts each point.

topspin
A way of hitting the ball so it spins forward, which in turn makes the ball bounce higher and deeper.

umpire
An official who enforces the rules during a tennis match.

volley
Hitting the ball before it hits the ground.

MORE INFORMATION

BOOKS

Monnig, Alex. *Serena Williams vs. Billie Jean King*. Minneapolis: Abdo Publishing, 2018.

Wells, Don. *Tennis*. New York: AV2 by Weigl, 2018.

ONLINE RESOURCES

To learn more about the GOATs of tennis, please visit **abdobooklinks.com** or scan this QR code. These links are routinely monitored and updated to provide the most current information available.

INDEX

ABOUT THE AUTHOR

Karen Price comes from a sports journalism background and covered hockey, baseball, and other fun pursuits during her time as a newspaper writer in Boulder, Colorado, and Pittsburgh, Pennsylvania. She is now a freelance writer and communications specialist who lives in Pittsburgh with her husband and three goofy cats.